"Since her first book, I've been a fan of Karen Enns. In *Dislocations* I'm delighted again with her precision with language, her musical ability to allow silence to sit among the words, her connection with the daily things going on around her. The poems are 'small mutinies' that quietly demand we live more fully and more generously in this sweet fragile world."
— LORNA CROZIER, author of *Through the Garden*

"Tuned to a cosmic lament, these poems shimmer and burn with beauty and loss." —CARLA FUNK, author of *Gloryland* and *Apologetic*

"Enns plays her phrases with precision, shapes haunting surprise. *Dislocations* is a candid concert for a grieving world."
— JANE MUNRO, author of *False Creek*

"Enns's work is masterful in its precision and joyful use of language. It is, like the sparkler she describes in a poem, 'lit, sizzling' with brilliance." —SARAH TSIANG, author of *Grappling Hook*

"The power of Enns's vision derives from her extraordinary ear, its exquisite sculpting of silence. Her free verse is among the most eloquent now being written in Canada." —JAN ZWICKY

"There is a sense, in this book, of something loosed—of a fine mind taking in the world and giving back to us something we didn't know we knew." —EVE JOSEPH, author of *In the Slender Margin*

"A compassionate voice is here at play within a world that is both uncanny and beautiful." —TIM LILBURN, author of *Kill-Site and Assiniboia*

"The world Karen Enns gives us is larger than we know, revealing a spaciousness we imagined gone. Hers is a resonant, fearless voice." —ANNE SIMPSON, author of *Speechless*

"Personal and remote, cool and exacting, mysteriously exciting, like a top skier these poems cut their own tracks." —GARY SNYDER, author of *This Present Moment*

OSKANA POETRY & POETICS

Karen Enns

Dislocations

![UP] University of Regina Press

Printed and bound in Canada at Imprimerie Gauvin. The text of this book is printed on 100% post-consumer recycled paper with earth-friendly vegetable-based inks.

Cover art: "Tree roots on white background" by dottedyeti /AdobeStock

Cover and text design: Duncan Campbell, University of Regina Press

Editor: Randy Lundy
Proofreader: Jellyn Ayudan

The text and titling faces are Arno, designed by Robert Slimbach.

Library and Archives Canada Cataloguing in Publication

Title: Dislocations / Karen Enns.

Names: Enns, Karen, 1960- author.

Series: Oskana poetry & poetics.

Description: Series statement: Oskana poetry & poetics ; 16 | Poems.

Identifiers: Canadiana (print) 20220446903 | Canadiana (ebook) 20220446938 | ISBN 9780889779303 (softcover) | ISBN 9780889779327 (EPUB) | ISBN 9780889779310 (PDF)

Classification: LCC PS8609.N66 D57 2023 | DDC C811/.6—dc23

10   9   8   7   6   5   4   3   2   1

UNIVERSITY OF REGINA PRESS
University of Regina
Regina, Saskatchewan
Canada S4S 0A2
TELEPHONE: (306) 585-4758
FAX: (306) 585-4699
WEB: www.uofrpress.ca
EMAIL: uofrpress@uregina.ca

We acknowledge the support of the Canada Council for the Arts for our publishing program. We acknowledge the financial support of the Government of Canada. / Nous reconnaissons l'appui financier du gouvernement du Canada. This publication was made possible with support from Creative Saskatchewan's Book Publishing Production Grant Program.

for Dave, Diane, and Rob, the children east of here

CONTENTS

v

I

TANNER RIDGE

From here, the farm could be a map
or a gameboard of neat squares.
Each square, fenced in, holds one horse,
each horse has one trough, one blanket
against the January cold.

A woman in a red jacket carries a red pail
and walks on the lane between the squares.
As she walks, each horse turns its head
to look after her, one by one.

It is so slight, the motion of each head
as she passes by with the red pail,
so slight an attention.

For a moment she is thought.
She is scent.

CLOVER POINT

This riot of gulls, the force
of these careening bodies,
hammering wings, this wind
ripping open the flaps of my coat
to make a sail of me,
could pelt me seaward, into the strait,
but I am held here, held to the point
by the notes of a ukulele,
yes, a small stringed instrument,
played by a man parked on the cliff
in his pickup, a man facing five bars of light
that come down to the sea,
reach right into it, five bars
almost hidden by cloud
so I have to look hard
to see the transformation of this day
into something other than a gap
between the past and the future,
other than a rift,
and so these song particles,
hardly arranged in a pattern at all,
riding the wind like tiny bleats
for a nanosecond each,
are enough.

LINEAGE

New houses will be going up past the back fence
where a man named Lou used to live alone,
used to sit and watch the deer run in circles
around his house. Wide circles,
as his lot was large for the suburbs,
unmanicured, you might say, left a little wild
for those deer: rampant ivy, salmonberry,
spreading mats of Oregon grape.
And Lou would watch the deer, content, he said,
because his wife had been content
watching too before she died,
watching the ancestors, maybe,
of the ones he watched now from his chair,
except his now has also passed
and it is mine, for a while,
as I watch the deer that Lou watched,
as his wife had watched,
the deer that are not the same
except from a distance.

GARDEN PARTY

The moon is orange tonight,
pure tangerine. It's the wildfires
to the north and east, we're told.
We see it through a canopy of fir
above our heads, as it moves along,
or as we do. As the conversation does,
which is steady, although random,
and less fervent than the candles
set in glasses on the table.
They, at least, flick arguments,
small mutinies into the dark.
But who will remember the words?
Those colourless moths
that swerve and disappear.
Not us. At midnight
we rise from our chairs,
adjust our sweaters and shawls,
and walk back
under the gist of orange
to where we were
before we spoke.

EAST OF HERE

1. The Canal

Listen long enough and something roars,
moves on its gargantuan axis,
creaks and groans. It isn't the ship
rising in the lock a mile from here, or the barns
settling down into the loam and clay,
and it isn't the wind that riffles the high grasses on the field,
the moving grasses behind the school
where the gulls lift off and flare above the creek
as they head for the strip of woods
east of here.

It isn't the bridge going up
to let the ship through the canal
as the schoolyard turns and turns in the belts of wind,
and the ship's horn blasts
and the gulls holler.

And it isn't you standing here,
listening hard. Not you.
You haven't lived yet.

2. Funnel

Spiral galaxy: a hundred billion stars
whose light takes fifty million years to reach me
standing here with a mug of tea
beside my climbing English rose, here in the garden
that belonged to a Spicer family when I still lived in Iowa,
a few miles east of rolling hills of corn, farms
that reminded me of the orchards of Niagara,
where one May night in '68 or '69
my father brought a sparkler home
for me to carry high, lit, sizzling,
as I ran across the lawn, and it mattered
that I held a single star in my hand.

3. *Long Thread, Lazy Girl*

What goes around comes around, they say,
as they hang the sheets on the line to dry.
As they bend over the quilts,
moving their needles in and out,
they say, Long thread, lazy girl.
As they punch down the dough in tubs,
they shake their heads and say,
Six days shalt thou work.
Scrubbing floors, darning socks,
picking beans, they say and say again
the words and nothing more.
And the shoes are polished,
the Sunday shirts ironed and hung,
the bread baked, the gardens hoed,
the hems taken down and stitched.

Be separate, they say, work and pray,
as they watch me from the row of spindly poplars
at the edge of the cemetery,
just past the thin wire fence
you can hardly see from here,
after which the orchard bends along the rise
and curves off over the next one,
out of sight, there,
where they stand in a group,
just there, in a little wind
that moves the leaves
across their faces.

4. After the Funeral

There were many in that small stucco house
beside a field and in the dark.
Many sitting on chairs around the rooms.
And God was there, they said, and I had seen His shape,
His hand, in the light around the lamps and polished tables,
the plates of food laid out.

I was nine. Upstairs, the window where I stood
was low enough to let the dark in, all of it,
its animal thickness, shifting, changing,
and the black leaves in the night scratched at the window
and moved in the trees over the field.
Moved over her as she rested on the current, rested
in her last resting, her thin hands folded on her chest,
the skirt close at her ankles, the black shoes tied,
her good blouse. But not the plaid shawl
she wore around her shoulders on summer evenings
when she sat outside in the yard. It could be,
couldn't it, hanging on the back of a chair
downstairs where the people were sitting.
Even in the wind that rasped the leaves, the eaves,
the window, her hair did not move, her brown hair
lay flat on her head. Just brown, just flat.
And then the eye. The glass one.

And while the people in the rooms below spoke softly
and were silent sometimes, most times,
and the pale light of Him watched over them,
she floated among the poplars,

not leaving or coming back. Quiet.
Still. As if she hadn't decided yet.
Or maybe it was Him. Or maybe
she was waiting for a kind of light
she would know to follow.

If she moved,
the eye might fall to the ground.
It might land on the lawn and keep seeing,
not from the side anymore,
but facing the sky, straight up.
Shining. And if you touched it, say,
if you picked a leaf off the grass in spring,
not knowing what lay underneath,
it would be cold.

5. The Hitchhiker

You walked up the lane to the barn one August noon,
young, dusty, looking for work. You didn't need a place
to stay, you said. Everything was in your pack.
The harvest was in full throttle, farmers on their orchard jeeps
hauling peaches up and down the gravel roads.
Talk in the barns as the sun dropped behind the canal every night
was all market prices, drought, bad help.
And into our lives you walked, a young Bacchus from a mythical world,
whistling a top-40 tune. Our lives, I say, meaning the ten of us,
or maybe twelve, working in the shed.
Women and girls in kerchiefs standing at the belt packing fruit,
hour after hour, day after day, passing the time with talk of nothing
we would remember later but a rhythm. A rise and fall
in the belt's slow churn. And in the silences?
We imagined our parallel lives, the ones that radiated out
from under the shed roof, out into the world,
bright with detail and dream.
You put up your tent behind the barn and early the next morning
went off with the pickers, harness dangling, grinning
and waving, swinging your legs off the tailgate.
We heard you used the hose behind the shed to shower off
before we came to work. Overlooking the valley at dawn,
shoulders, arms, tanned and smooth, was how we pictured you,
a pink sun just visible behind the church across the creek,
the sky already pale with haze.

If you read this now, you might remember a summer of travelling,
stopping at a farm to work a couple of weeks. You might remember
light-haired girls in the packing shed and unrelenting heat

in the orchards. How you pitched your tent
at the edge of a valley, above the rows of young pear trees,
the makeshift shower there. How you came and went.
That's what we remember. You with your accent,
a sleek, dark gift, how you left one morning for the highway,
your hair dripping water from the tap
like you'd been baptized, called to another life
after forty days and nights in the desert.

6. Thrift

In the old tiled kitchen,
I cracked eggs into a bowl.
Scrape your thumb around the shell,
my mother said, to get it all. Like this.
When I asked her why, she said,
Because they didn't have enough.
The women. All the women didn't have enough.
Enough egg, enough bread, milk, soup,
potatoes. Their teeth fell out.
Their bones broke. Their tears
stopped falling on the hands of their children.
Out of respect, still,
I am careful with eggs.

7. Closed Universe

Look into the distance, we were told,
focus on the narrow corridor of light ahead.
Do not let your attention drift, they said.

Do not waver.

At first the entrance will seem small,
as small as the eye of a needle,
but it will widen gradually
and open and keep opening into everything,
blamelessness and beauty, bliss,
radiance, and it will not end.

This is what they said.

But we must have veered.
We were distracted.

There were instances difficult to ignore.
The sound of singing, once or twice. Some complications
on the periphery. A few wild notions of colour and shape.

And then there were the hesitancies
around direction and loop.

And here we are

at a vision of the backs of our heads, the napes
of our necks, the small cowlicks there.

8. In All These Poems

In all these poems
I'm partly somewhere else.
With you, without you,
walking toward you or away,
but you are there, your small face
watching from the shadow of a doorway
or a set of stairs, from behind a curtain or a table.
Sometimes I see you at the piano.
You stop playing, turn to me,
and in that pause,
tell me something necessary.

II

A MESSAGE

The real words exist, we're told,
and they are precise beyond belief.
But they are not here—
not in this poem,
or in any other.

We walk on hard ground, frost-covered, clotted,
an atlas of what's already been.

And then there is this: the air is thin,
unknowable, not kind.

       Who can sleep?

We dream of dark, crouching birds, small
and smaller rooms, inconsistencies of meaning in the walls,

     voices, voices

       conjugating infinite verbs.

Deft. It was deft
the way brilliance was heaped on us,

through leaves like that,

distilled, too much
                and not enough at once,

                                every detail

charged with a pizzicato intelligence.

You could say it was blinding, but it wasn't.

There were visions in the under-pitch,
                slow reverberations.

Without which the moment flattens out
and spreads, becomes the length and width

of one endless night.

This one,

rattling its tail of bristles.

Without which, meaning love,
meaning,

without love

dawn will be difficult.

What we know now is less disclosed
than what we knew before.

We could walk on water then, couldn't we?
Slabs of transparency,

                              solid amazement.

Overtones of light splintered the surface
as if it were glass

                and ringing.

In those days
we entered a valley we thought could be named.

Spreading forms of shadow tailed us.
Thinning forms appeared ahead, leading
or retreating,

      it was hard to tell.

Spikes of fern among the rock alerted us
to gashes in the air

      that would not heal.

We wanted a say
but nothing came out of our mouths.

And there were other things.

Death, for instance.

Liturgies falling from the trees,
fragments of psalms, proverbs.

Ecclesiastes: ash on our tongues.

Revelations: a form of wind.

The ratio of love to grief
we understood as music.

Lyricism as proportion.

The steady rise and fall of quantity
set against the possibility of sway.

It was a kind of cumulus.

Every time,
something bloomed and disappeared.

Beauty has burned itself out at the edges.
It is so obvious.

A charred clarity,
        the smell of sweet tinder.

All we can mouth in the after-heat are vowels.

But the nights are cool.
In the dark, we finger five-star consonants.

To imagine a colour no one has seen.

And then

white anemones among the cedar.

See how carefully we move,
   with such tenderness.

Only our bare souls remain.

Our phantom limbs

   sense everything.

III

> *It is during that return, that pause,*
> *that Sisyphus interests me.*
> —ALBERT CAMUS

Now that the boulder has thundered down the mountain
to land at the base where it sits between two trees
in the brilliant heat,
    and the air is clear of the dust churned up
    with its plunge,

and the crows that spewed black and jagged from the underbrush
at the noise of the great rock going down,
have settled once again on the gorse
as if nothing has happened, as if the day has simply gone on
as it does
under the broiling sun,

    he picks his way down in his sandals.

This is the time.

This is the time he can notice things.

There are succulents, for instance, growing in the crevices,
    wafers of moisture hidden in their coral-tipped pads,
and tufts of scorched grass through which grey-green lizards
    whip out and scatter.

He can finger tiny sprouts of lichen on the ledges,
and study the paths of warblers in the soft dust
that covers the trail he has made.

He remembers every detail,

but the light is different. Each time
        the light is different.

And although he knows the descent,
although he knows each cleft in the rock, each footing,
each give and hardness, rise and drop, the ragged mouth
of a cave,

the olive trees that spread on the bitter slopes,
that say, here, they say to him, here,
                        this is the way of return,

he wonders still,
                he wonders
at the deference of the mountain.

But things have been said. All things.

At the low rock wall he squats
and then lies fully on the pebbled ground
                        in the eave of its shade.
Lies against the last wedge of the last coolness
of the last darkness.

Bliss he thinks
        or feels, as there is no division in him now.

When he opens his eyes, the sky is the blue of the sea below him.
The shape of a fishing village in the distance
has remained a shape, the hills remained the shape of hills,

and in the lobes of lichen and succulent, in the architecture of the ledges,
the dry bark of a magpie on the ridge,
   on a twig,
    on the wall,

there is mercy.

But everything has been said.

And now he can see where the great pock-marked boulder
rests between two trees.

He reaches it and touches the surface,
traces with his fingers the pitted sum of what it has been
since the beginning, the accumulated
heat and cold,
   its mineral age,

and readies himself for the push.

His hands are strong. His shoulders braced.
His cheek meets the hot stone.
He begins.

Having gorged, white-plumed,
over stones of indigo, grey, maroon,
the river cuts its way down, drops farther,
farther down, and farther
into a quiet pool reflecting ferns.

Only a hint of turbulence remains
in a small curl of current
circling the tip of a branch
half-submerged near my hand.
This, as a bloom of cirrus
slides across the surface of its soul.

It wasn't the shore that caught my eye,
pale, scalloped as the tide came in,
but a flash on the periphery,
a group of geese, seven or eight,
in the shallows.

Then again, to be precise,
it wasn't the geese that glimmered and flared,
but the water next to them, the water
they stirred.

A brilliance opened and closed
and opened again.
And when I left, still early, still dawn,

I carried an image,
not of the geese themselves
or their movements, the tide coming in,
or the stretch of shore,

but of flickering. Nothing solid.

The point, the whole point,
might have been the white-dust trailhead.
It might have been the whiskey jacks that weighed down
the limbs of the trees up there.

It might have been the solitude.

But something moved in the dark water of the stream
under my hand. It moved.
Something soft in the cold water
between smooth stones.

It might have been that.

Massive, moss-covered firs lie across the forest floor
as if they have fallen here lightly,

made hardly a sound going down,
        hardly a sound as they landed.

In the open space beyond their grounded canopies,
absence, you could say unwooded-ness,
        a species of grief,

the light on its own there,
and the last echo of the trees going down.

A few shafts flare through, toward me
and toward the other woman who walks by on the trail.

Elusive, she says as she passes,
and I think she means the barred owls calling out
from behind the ridge, off to one side,
then the other,

always invisible, moving,
moving in the upper storeys.

        But maybe she means time,
        which can't be right.

Here,
at the fir-beginnings, white-cut,
at eye level,

it is pure and circular.

MIDDENS, GORDON HEAD

She emerges naked from a cleft in the rock
and wades into the sea, her body white
in the post-noon haze, a slender heron wing
against the dark water of the cove.
I see her from the cliff above the middens
where the yellow trail disintegrates.
Behind us, smoke from burning forests
has stunted the city, blunted cloud and skylines.
Ahead, the desiccated hills of San Juan rim the strait.
She does not see me, the young woman,
but neither does she look,
and this makes the moment fine, so fine,
the moment of her smooth glide into the sea
without a glance around her.
She turns her body to the apocalyptic light
and floats on the surface of the deepest dark
that holds her. How much we have lost.
How much is shattered, is interrupted
by her small, white form
suspended under plains of ash.

PLATEAU

On a ridge near the summit,
Garry oaks sprawl like aging sentinels,
mystics cowled with moss.

Something breathes without a sound up here,
sleeps with one eye open.
Something doesn't sleep.

ISLAND VIEW BEACH

A month of steps.
The tide recedes and leaves
a shell-studded prairie.
Cliffs across the strait
barometer the light
that scalds their surfaces.
Some kind of glory burns.

GEESE

Their calls seem almost human
as they come across the fields,
first one, then a few more,
but not many in the last of this dusk.
As if they've suddenly awakened from a long sleep
to a world stunned by falling grey.
What sudden flatness,
what effort to lift the body into it.
As the wind of their muscled rise
hits the low perimeter,
what grief articulated there,
what lamentation.

IV

Dogwoods are blooming all over the city,
and the ash trees at the back fence shimmer
with something new and fine. Those days too,
the aspens were shaking; young larches flickered and flared
beside the northern highways on the way to Edmonton.
At the windows of the car, your small faces
turned to timberlines and cut banks, a herd of caribou once,
a wolf, miles of foothills and scrub, glacial lakes
that opened turquoise after hairpin curves.
And in the cabins off the main route, early mornings in bed,
all of us in a row, quilts around us, over us,
under, the chill air of the mountains
in our hair and on our shoulders, yours
so thin-boned still, bird-like,
so tenuous against the aspens
almost white with turning now, highways
faded into the passes, the caribou herd
pale in a riverbed streaked with drought.

The four of them are sitting on the grass,
bare-legged, in a clump, not posed exactly,
gathered, you could say. It is obviously summer.
Everything is shining, green, beyond the light on them.
They sit together in its circle: three small bodies,
boys (one has a missing tooth),
around a larger body, a woman's, her skirt
bunched up around her thighs, her arm around the one,
a hand stretched flat across his ribcage.
You can see she wears a watch. Gold.
Probably a gift.

There are other hands in various positions,
on a shoulder, on a lap.
Two hands in the front are caught in a moment
of rubbing together, palm to palm,
possibly rolling something very small
between them. Something red?
A berry or a flower bud, or so it seems.
A marble? Hard to tell.
Some of the hands are hidden in the grass
on which a few Arbutus leaves have fallen much too early,
and behind a back, a leg.
The small knees in the front are dirty and scratched.
Another knee in the shade behind them
is also dark, partly due to the shadow,
but likely a matter of dirt as well.

And the photographer's hands are also hidden.
The face as well, the body.
But you can see him in the faces of the four of them.
He is the one they're smiling at.
He and the aperture.

NOT EXACTLY DAWN

At not exactly dawn,
the numbness in the streets
holds the early click and shudder of sparrows
                              at a distance.

The shortcut through the park is endless,
windows of the houses on the border
have drawn back into walls.

The last air is breathed out of the city,
                              or almost.

And the walk through the back gate to the house,
through the garden, past the apple tree
and up the back steps
by the trellis is imagined,
                              or delayed, or both.

There is no way to know for certain.
All coming light is paralyzed.

NIGHT SOUNDS

The sounds you hear in the night
might very well be them, those past selves
crowding in, jostling elbows, shoulders,
although gently, as many are frail with age.
The younger ones, emotional at times,
are more likely to hold vigils, candlelit,
at which they chant or sing in unison.
Sometimes prayers are said, invocations
to the gods or history or to you, especially
when nostalgia hits them hard. Early evenings, dawns.
The more political of them have signed petitions,
in some cases started protests,
never violent, but with a quiet urgency
that leaves you shaking with love.
But it is momentary, on your part at least;
they have been, it must be said, left behind.
Some accept rejection better than others.
A straggler here and there can be seen eating ice cream
on a park bench, sipping a glass of wine,
or reading a book of poems in a hammock.
But in general they are not at peace.
Their eyes, through which you seem remote,
or worse, dismissive, are beseeching.
Their hands, so much smaller than your own,
drift at their sides wanting to carry something for you,
be of help. They have nothing to do after all,
but lift their voices to the indifferent air.
Yes, they can be heard to say amongst themselves,
nodding to each other. Yes, they say, as a group,
more fervently. We were relevant. We lived.

HEIDI, FIRST SNOW

We sit here in the quiet of a morning that has no purpose
and, now, dwindling angles. The hedge is hilled, the planters
sloped. A junco skips across what used to be the patio.

At the window, you keep watch, your Shepherd ears
flipped up and keen to sounds of falling only you can decipher.
Frequencies of drift, near-silence. The brief inhalations of cedars.

And here too, distinctions. The book on my lap lies open.
Something about grief and resignation on the page,
patterns of loss and leave-taking. Undulating layers of reflection.

What about these layers, I ask your profile at the window.
Your response is measured, taking in the complexities.
You turn to me, tilt your head, lift the delicate ridge of your brow.

Anything could happen. A revelation, for instance,
appear in print, almost readable, on the fine strip of pearl
at the edge of the earth. Or this could be a day
on which every door is closed in your face.
The walls could echo with the sound of barking dogs,
the floor shake with rumblings of a train.
Sunlight could streak through the blinds early,
or late, toward evening, or the sky offer nothing
but cloud and a sense of evasion. Be vigilant.
A crow could land on the sill where the paint is peeling,
and speak to you in sentences so finely crafted
you accept the message as good news from another realm.
Or someone playing Chopin one street over, windows open,
could be really good, and the elegant betrayals of metre
clear the fences, oblivious to bylaws and borders.
Or the day could go on as it usually does. Mullings.
Procrastinations. You deadhead geraniums in the faded pots;
study the lizards invading the patio, and on a hunch,
the foundation for cracks; you check the trellis for wear
under the weight of clematis that's overshot all estimates of growth.
And when night comes down completely,
you cross the street. You scan the eucalyptus tree,
the only one on the block, and see the resident owl
perched on a mid-level branch, alert for signs
of the smallest transformation.
Darkness tilts the universe.
You hear a shift.

IN DREAM: APPEARANCES

I'm impatient with the fox, its black nosing
over and over the composted earth,
how it abandons its coverings, finally, its mask,
in the gully hidden by sumac and ash,
and shakes out a private sleekness there,
the burnished tail, the haunches.
Hunkered down on the periphery
among the tamped-down leaves,
I take in its gleaming teeth. I wait,
but I am not the enemy, which is to say,
my eyes are not hard gems.
I do not calculate.
I'm invested in an exchange.
If it too sees me, sees me watching,
if it snares my scent, I will know
I am here. I exist.

An hour of digging, grappling with sleeves and gloves,
roots and thorns, and the tooth-grinding clang of the spade
blade hitting stone or a long-buried bone.
A rage in me at the heat that ricochets
off the white stucco walls of the house.
And there is grief and an undercurrent of shame.
But that comes later, as the image sharpens.
Human wrestling with an intricate biosystem.
Human, triumphant, pulling a small shrub from the soil.
Human grieving as she considers the rose,
cut from its home district, its rich, bacterially complex,
root-sensed, musk-tunnelled, humus-walled,
loam-sweet continent.

THREE POEMS FOR 2021

I

The streets are empty except for the banners,
thin, half-torn, hanging from the sides of buildings.
Whatever they were meant to celebrate is now irrelevant.
Nothing helped, we tell ourselves, the banners tell us,
everything's been done.
A child riding by on a bicycle just now
would revive us all, or a magnolia in full bloom.
Come to think of it, those delicate pastel silks
could save us lyrically. I mean,
we could lose ourselves, couldn't we,
in a rhapsody so finely tuned,
our hearts open enough
to let in slender riffs.

II

You people celebrating on the barges
roped together in the middle of the inlet
seem oblivious. Hello out there! The night is over.
This is a new year, revellers, not a residue.
Your music, from here on the bridge, sounds stale.
A cigarette butt on the sidewalk of another era.
And it isn't only a matter of distance.
An echo of celebration or love or some kind of nostalgia
reverberates across the water, fair enough,
but the aftersound is metal,
faint scratches on an empty can.

III

And so the long year begins.
We have no recourse here,
the scavenged light is at our eyes.
Dissent has faded from the trees,
faint protestations from the soil.
We step toward imagined towns
in emerald valleys, the sound
of running water. New rivers
or the old ones coming back.

We hear their calls from the kitchen.
A gangly arrow of them headed for the strait.

Maybe over water
they'll experiment with shape
or sound or ritual.
Maybe they'll absorb a notion of formlessness
and separate.
There might be violence
or lethargy,
a slight drop in altitude
and morale,

an insistence, finally,
on privacy.

GIVE ME YOUR WORD

They are less than visions, fragments,
faint displacements I barely hear,
the trailing off of echoes like falling leaves.

And time? The light just flickers there.

Give me your word that these peripheries,
these floaters that form musics in the space behind my eyes,
come together in the end. Tell me
their fonts, their strokes and pitches,
the tiny particulate blooms,
are integral to some luminescent whole.

I've held my ear to the ground as I was told.
I've listened to the modulations of my age,
been exile and participant at once, a keeper
of resonance and swirl, of emptiness, too.

And I have been amazed.

But it remains. You must have known how this would be.
It overtakes me, breathes, this instinct, this agility,
the move toward synchronicity and home.

IN THE PARKING LOT

The old man sitting in the sun,
leaning on the wall beside his bicycle,
his bags of stuff, shakes his head
as I park to run into the grocery
for soap and lettuce, cheese.
My car, you see, straddles the solid line,
the one that tells you to stay in your own place,
that tells you not to add disorder to the parking lot
or worse, the world, but I have,
and the old man leaning on the warm wall
of the sandwich shop knows this,
understands the risk of it, the jolt.
I apologize to him, keeper of the lot,
for this and more, but he only shrugs.
It'll pass in the dark, he says.

I'd like to tell you something from this side of the hedge.
The sky is wide open for conduct, after all,
and molecules of nitrogen stand by as messengers.
But though this poem clears the hedge,
it might not have the tenacity, the coalescing power,
to keep itself intact. It might not thrive.
Lines could come apart out there in the ether,
separate and separate again, waft off, meaning with them,
syntax unravel as the pull of public gravity,
that sober, grounding force, unpacks the lift.
It's only here, on this side, that the vision stays precise.
A private mime plays out against the dark green cedar.
If I look closely and the sun is bright,
I see a certain lilt, small stepping motions
as the feet of words move subtly
and with grace.

QUESTIONS FOR A MUSE

What if I was wrong?
If after years of creeping away
for mere minutes in your peculiar half-dusk,
half-dream, your endless edge,
after standing in doorways and laneways,
in kitchens and carports and schoolyards,
waiting for a chance to slip away to you,
I misread the cues?

Because you're here now,
and this desk, this chair are free,
and there is time,
but you are cool, so cool,
and your voice, almost inaudible,
is not generous, not soothing
or melodic. Honestly,
at times you seem tone-deaf.
Or is it me?

The trees that ring the house are quiet,
the door is closed, the refrigerator
hums at its usual pitch.
Can't we have a conversation, be friendly,
get to know each other better?
Do you have a vulnerable side, for instance?

And just now: Can you hear it?
The white-throat singing in the hedge,
singing and singing as if for the first time.

There is nothing between the tips of your fingers
and the keys. Not even charged air.
But the hammer felts are tamped down,
worn thin with intent and transfer.
Look under the lid, he says.

You are not the beginning of the long, long gesture,
the extension through nine feet of string.
You are not the source. You are the middle.
The beginning was a pressure.

Your wrist is the problem. No,
it's your shoulder. Ah, I see now,
it must be your neck.
Play as if for the last time.
As if your body is not necessary,
it cannot be.

Minor is the other side of major.
The turned coin, the shadow.
Remember: *duende*.
The semi-tone drop is the fall of an angel.

The *lied* is finely balanced. Singer and pianist
in lyric conversation. Why are you
slumped over the keys like that?
Why is glass breaking in the other room
as the soprano's dress heaves?

My time will come, said Mahler once.
This is the artist's life.
Believe. Believe. Believe.
Then die.

You are too young to play this piece.
You have not lived enough. Or listened long enough
to single drops of water land on stone.
What is necessary happens between each sound.
Your life that thinned out, that rhythmic.

Play Debussy with your skin.
Schumann, Schubert, your heart.
Shostakovich? Play with your nerves.
But steel them. They are black wires
in a lightning storm.

You are the fugue. Yes, you.
The voices, all of them, are yours,
your polyphonic self.
No damper pedal needed.
You sustain them all.

Unless you sacrifice belongings, maps, your shoes,
that coat there on the chair,
the other realm is only tantalizing.
Poverty, a stream of hard need, brings it in close.

Can sound be this pristine, this caught?
Yes. Each pitch is an elevated sphere.
Suspended. Think *appoggiatura*.
The radiance of rise and delay.

In a hundred hours of practice,
only a few will reach that far edge of bliss.
The loop back. There, at the top of the arc,
where the tension is exquisite.

Whatever it takes. Desire. Melancholy. Anger.
Too much joy is a problem. Too much grief
is not. A balance is ridiculous.
Never use red ink on your score.

If you can't shape this phrase, give up.
You are not an artist. Not a pianist. Barely human.
This is where you die or choose to live.
Dying is the more expressive of the two.
Now begin.

Listen with the third ear.
The one you reach for in the night.
That one, perfectly tuned,
a moon in the solid dark.
It hears each note as if it were a continent.

No one will actually dance to this,
but Bartók sends you an invitation. Accept.
The pulse is remembered. From when?
Earlier. Where? The feet, of course.

On a summer night like this one,
only nocturnes. *Rubato*, absence.
No talk. The left hand keeps time
while the right digresses.
Open the window. There is so much loss.

The finest pull. To notice every detail, backlit,
brilliant, and nothing at all. To be dazzled
and lost at once. This is performance.

See how the phrase spins on an axis.
It is all about geometry.
Listen for the complicity, the shift,
the elegant proof.

No score. The music is now in your mind,
arranged in segments and strata. But the final synthesis
shimmers offstage, whole and soundless.
You might hear it from the bench,
but this is unlikely. We can hope.

Brahms: the final opus.
The end of translation. A signing off of its spirit.
Wait for the tenderness. *Dolce. Pianissimo.*
The leaf drifts to earth.
Each vein holds all living in it one last time.

Those poplars in Iowa, a stand of them
at the edge of a park I have no name for and walked through only once,
taking a gravel path I didn't know toward a street
unfamiliar to me,

those poplars come back,
        keep coming back.

In the evenings usually, as I cook,
as I sort the vegetables and chop them on the wooden board,
peel the onions, garlic, choose the peppers, rinse the celery,
tomatoes, and there they are, the poplars,
        sudden,
           with a wind in them,
                coltish almost,
                all limbs and ribs,

picking up and shirring the leaves, shirring the time it takes me
to walk by, turning it over and over and over, gathering it in,

        and the sound of the shifting, lifting leaves,
crossing and re-crossing, thousands of leaves
intersecting thousands of times,
thousands of nerve-slivers pitched in the air
like a music of something will happen,
will happen
        happen,
something will happen,

and I don't know what it can be,
I don't know until later,
and later still,
as I arrange the vegetables in rows on the wooden board
and think I will slice the onions next
before I add the oil, add the salt,
        I wonder,
        what was it anyway?

The something that arrived
was only more,
more of whatever was in the leaves,
                the air, the park,
more of whatever
was shaking me then,
more of the question.

Here you are among hydrangeas on steroids,
pumped up for the sale,
looking out at the crumbling shed, which seemed,
when you saw it first, quaint, but now a project,
and all your lovely junk.
Paper documents of acquisitions and defeats, files,
forks, photographs, children's art, now dimpled with time
and a long fridge span—who said, you never know
who might become the next Picasso?—not to mention
the broken yellow bicycle in the dining room,
curtain rods that may or may not fit the curtains you have yet to buy,
a piano on loan, beds the wrong size for the rooms
and the people in them, empty plastic pots
for the perennials you meant to divide
but left behind in your garden, the old one,
to keep watch for you, your claim from beyond,
and books. Boxes of books. More books than necessary
to flesh out the tale of your obsessions.
Russian winters, South African nights, post-war
displacements, moors and heaths, grey Slavic cities
in relentless rain, plains and solitude,
poplars, and more plains, Irish,
Spanish, northern coasts,
and now the moving truck pulls away
like a train out of a station built beyond the treeline.
Coal for lamps. Little food.
The neighbourhood as silent as snow.

Tomorrow you'll notice
the mourning dove here out-mourns the gulls
that swooped above the other house.
A single note of grief can hold within its pitch
the overtones of many. And you,
standing in the hall, holding a jar of metal screws
brought over from the old basement
but there isn't one here so you carry them,
you can almost hear each one.

VARIATIONS

I want to know what she knows at the end,
as the leaves clatter down around her bed,
and the barn door opens and closes
with a wind from the north.
I want to know what she sees
through the curtains then, if anything.
Filtered light, a shadow of elm.
Pale details of the variations on a theme.

ORDINARY

You singing in the next room.
Swells of baritone, colourful banners
in a parade going by.

Light on the cedar hedge
that the neighbour points out
has died inside. Just look, he says.

The distant drone of traffic below the ridge
heading to the ferry every morning.

My cup on the sill,
although not the blue one I loved,
which cracked one winter.

A pencil left on the table
last week or possibly the week before.

Bits of fern on the carpet near the door
as if there has been a flutter of leaving.

EARLY JANUARY

You sparrows,
                    chittering away,
now at the eaves, now at the feeder,

now snipping tapers of wisteria,
dangling from the trellis;

you chipping crowd of tribe-beings,
with your bulb bellies tucked in,

do you think in collage?

Your tiny brains must be compound lenses
snapping leaf vein,
        seed pod,
            bud tip,
                shadow tip,

wordless,
must be needle points of thought-patter
zipping at a bird-light speed.

Little whizzers, little blips,
I have a practical concern:

the shadows of your quick jibbing
flicker on the window glass between us,
        and interrupt my longer gaze,
longer line,
longer reach,

your trills,

           your upper, lower throat-mordents
seal the argument
for short blasts of bliss

against a horizontal focus,

and now,
now that you've made your point,
           you've quipped off,

leaving me in silence,
         and the spirals of wisteria

       swinging.

TERCE

Above the lavender, stale with winter now and crisp,
ornamental grasses hold a spindly stance against the wind.
This low sea house has no place in the grey enormity.
Gulls give it points of light, a reference,
in this middle morning hour.
And who are you in this place
that has no place beside the sea,
in this hour that has no time? Who are you
in this silence among the sage and burnt-out lavender?
Do the gulls lend you a point as well, a voice?
You would say no, you would claim irrelevance
from your chair at the window.
And when a band of stratus splits over the water,
and the mouth of it almost speaks to you,
almost says what you wish you could say
if you had a language for it,
here at this selvage edge of the world,
of your life, you have proof.

ALMOST

There is nothing to say.
Deer graze near the white house again,
their shapes barely moving under the trees.
In the shadows there.
Nothing else is moving. No wind.
There has never been wind it seems,
never so many things.
But belief. There is that.
And music.
Some days nothing becomes something
and then nothing again.
You read the lips of air.

ACKNOWLEDGEMENTS

My sincere thanks to Randy Lundy for the editorial
fine-tuning that helped shape this collection.

A warm thank you to Eve Joseph, Patricia Young, and Patrick
Friesen for conversations and support along the way. A special
note of gratitude to Jan Zwicky for close reading and commentary.

Versions of several poems have previously appeared in
The New Quarterly ("Lineage," as "Oregon Grape," and
"Garden Party"), *Vallum Magazine* ("Not Exactly Dawn"),
Prairie Fire ("After the Funeral" and "Tanner Ridge"),
Grain Magazine ("Clover Point"), and *Anthropocene*
("Witness" and "Geese"). My thanks to the editors.

I would like to acknowledge the support of the BC Arts Council.

And to my dear family, including the youngest members, a
heartfelt thank you for inspiration and enthusiasm.

Karen Enns is the author of three books of
poetry: *Cloud Physics*, winner of the Raymond
Souster Award, *Ordinary Hours*, and *That Other
Beauty*. She lives in Victoria, British Columbia.

ᐅᓈᐸ

OSKANA POETRY & POETICS
BOOK SERIES

Publishing new and established authors, Oskana Poetry
& Poetics offers both contemporary poetry at its best
and probing discussions of poetry's cultural role.

Randy Lundy—*Series Editor*

Advisory Board

Sherwin Bitsui	Tim Lilburn
Robert Bringhurst	Duane Niatum
Laurie D. Graham	Gary Snyder
Louise Bernice Halfe	Karen Solie

PREVIOUS BOOKS IN THE SERIES:

Measures of Astonishment: Poets on Poetry,
presented by the League of Canadian Poets (2016)

The Long Walk, by Jan Zwicky (2016)

Cloud Physics, by Karen Enns (2017)

The House of Charlemagne, by Tim Lilburn (2018)

Blackbird Song, by Randy Lundy (2018)

Forty-One Pages: On Poetry, Language and Wilderness,
by John Steffler (2019)

Live Ones, by Sadie McCarney (2019)

Field Notes for the Self, by Randy Lundy (2020)

Burden, by Douglas Burnet Smith (2020)

Red Obsidian, by Stephan Torre (2021)

Pitchblende, by Elise Marcella Godfrey (2021)

Shifting Baseline Syndrome, by Aaron Kreuter (2022)

Synaptic, by Alison Calder (2022)

The History Forest, by Michael Trussler (2022)